DEVELOPING
EMPLOYEES

Enhancing Employee Performance

REGINALD HAYES

ISBN: 1-4196-9388-3
ISBN-13: 9781419693885

Visit www.booksurge.com to order additional copies.

TABLE OF CONTENTS

Defining Employee Development
Chapter One

Employee development can be defined as the art of improving and increasing the skill level of an individual or group of individuals, which leads toward the positive growth in their general, technical, and leadership skills. It is the art of taking a neophyte from being a participant to being a major contributor to the organization's goals and objectives. Several things must occur to make this happen: one, you must provide proper orientation; two, you must provide the necessary tools, such as computers, supplies, office equipment, etc.; and three, you must serve as a mentor or provide one to help the neophyte along his or her way. If you fail at these three things, you make it easy for the employee to fail at achieving maximum efficiency within the organization.

Designing Training Programs
Chapter Two

There are several methods used in providing training to employees. The primary methods are classroom instruction, distance learning, including satellite broadcasting, Webcasting and other forms of e-learning such as Net meetings, online education programs, and others. What works best depends on the individual. The past five years have led me to believe that most trainees prefer classroom instruction—where interaction can occur between the student and the instructor—second to satellite broadcasting. While e-learning, including Webcasting and live meetings, is less expensive and newer than other forms of training and instruction, it loses people if they do not maintain a functional grasp of computer technology and a general familiarity with the various software applications available to the learning community. Training programs must be designed to fit different groups of learners, as one size does not fit all. An effective instructional designer can develop learning modules that reflect the needs of a specific audience, all the more reason that agencies and private industry should canvass the market thoroughly prior to settling with one contractor versus another. Cost is another important factor in this equation. The best proposal is not always from the lowest bidder when delivering training to your organization. It is important to review each factor and its direct and indirect impact on the course and its participants. On occasion, you will settle for a higher cost estimate from a private contractor or consultant who better addresses the proposal's requirements and demonstrates the ability to meet the deliverables as required in the statement of work. A good statement of work contains a clear set of tasks with target dates for delivery of the required products. Take an extra moment to review the training proposal against the overall needs of the course and the organization it is designed for.

Instructional Needs
of Career Employees

Chapter Three

An effective way of gathering the training needs of your employees is through a needs assessment. The assessment should contain employees' titles, general and technical competencies for being successful in the positions, and a learning plan that defines the training courses that, in all probability, will enhance overall job performance. It is advisable for a supervisor and manager to meet with their subordinates frequently to decide on what resources are available to enhance employee performance. The fact is that, at times, the employee and manager become so familiar with one another over the course of employment that it may appear that no training, formal or informal, is required to improve job performance. This is not true. It has been demonstrated that employees receiving training on an ongoing basis do better in their job responsibilities while feeling better and more confident in what they do. This is all the more reason to provide regular training to staff members to advance their job competencies and capabilities. Assessments can be accomplished in a variety of ways. One, you can use an electronic or manual survey tool to record the training needs of your employees or you can simply track and schedule their training based on observation alone.

The bottom line is that you must do this regularly with emphasis on what their job competencies call for. Additionally, an evaluation tool must be developed to track the growth and performance of employees. Using methods devised by training guru Donald L. Kirkpatrick, at a minimum you should evaluate the employees' training at four levels, including: reaction, how those who participate in the program react to it; learning, the extent to which employees change attitudes, improve knowledge, and/or increase skills; behavior, the extent to which changes in behaviors have occurred; and results, the final results that occurred because the participants participated in the program.

Managing People
Chapter Four

Great leadership starts with looking at yourself—who you are and what you stand for. Leaders must learn to clearly convey their points of view. If not, how can they expect subordinates to effectively implement the assignments given to them? People like to see into the heart of their leaders–to know that they're working for a good person, someone they can trust. Without trust, employees feel defeated before they get started. It is incumbent upon a manager and supervisor to set the stage, a stage on which there is equal and full interaction between them and those who make their assignments.

People have a natural instinct to size up their superiors in terms of predicting performance outcomes. As their job performance rests with the perceptions of another human being, they become intimately concerned with how they are viewed by their leadership long before the actual performance evaluation period occurs. They want to know what in their behaviors and job competencies means the most to those having a career impact on their lives.

It is not difficult for a good manager to accept these concerns on the part of employees they supervise, if that manager practices a 360-degree evaluation process. What this means is that an employee should have the opportunity to evaluate his or her manager with the same amount of impact as the manager has. What happens is in today's world is that the leadership of organizations, particularly government agencies, does not trust or, in some cases, value the opinions of subordinate staff, which continues to perpetuate a lopsided evaluation process. Leadership must continue to find better ways to evaluate employee performance to arrive at a true assessment of how well they are meeting the goals and objectives of people who work for them. The process is perpetual; it does not stop at the manager-to-employee level. It must carry over into the employee-to-manager level as well if we are to experience a true 360-degree evaluation methodology.

Sometimes you may feel overwhelmed as a supervisor or manager. Perhaps you have had little or no training in how to be a successful manager. Maybe you want a refresher course on management covering all the latest information on essential management strategies. Without the right kind of training, the role of manager/supervisor can seem overwhelming, requiring you to juggle multiple priorities and demands.

In government, the job can be especially challenging. You often must be able to help staff members deal with constant changes, budget cuts, staff reductions, and wage freezes. This is in addition to the normal responsibilities of performance management, delegation, team development, coaching, and conflict resolution. You balance the role of leader, coach, cheerleader, and scorekeeper all in the midst of constant changes and shifting priorities.

Establishing Employee Work Plans

Chapter Five

A best practice in structuring goals and objectives for employees is through the use of an annual work plan. A work plan serves as the primary performance objective to meet individual and group assignments during a specific performance period. It is important to include any and all expectations that the employee is responsible for in the work plan document. It should be designed prior to the performance period with input from each employee and communicated to the group initially with quarterly reminders and updates during the year. Without a written work plan, it becomes difficult for some employees to track individual and group responsibilities. The manager relinquishes formal control over critical assignments, as he or she may also fail to remember important tasks at the end of the performance period.

The plan should be divided into columns listing the responsible person, tasks, target completion dates, actual completion dates, status column, and comments.

The plan should be discussed and modified as needed between the manager and employee during the year. This tool also allows a manager to add new assignments as given by superiors during the twelve-month period. It is recommended that each employee take responsibility for updating work plan assignments quarterly. This way, if modifications are required, they can be made prior to the close of the performance period. Granted, those in leadership can operate without such a document; however, they run the risk of disabling their ability to complete an accurate employee assessment during midyear and annual reviews.

Annual Performance Plans
Chapter Six

A good annual performance plan includes critical elements and standards expected of the employee, giving consideration to the number of required tasks, number of employees completing the tasks, level of difficulty relative to each task, and other factors, such as funding available to complete each task. For instance, an employee having contractor support to effectively implement a requirement stipulated in the annual work plan has a better chance of completing the tasks sooner and more effectively than one who has no funding at all. Supervisors must take this into account when assigning tasks and ultimately evaluating employees on overall performance. Funding permits outsourcing and procurement assistance that yields additional staff support and allows additional resources to get the job done. Some have made the mistake of thinking that funding doesn't matter, which creates a false sense of success between various employees, those with funding assistance and those without. In this regard, more training is required of those supervisors who may engage in this practice.

While companies and government agencies have grievance procedures to address disparities in employee performance, some are used more effectively than others. In some cases, private companies require employees to use private legal resources, which, in many cases, are unaffordable for employees, particularly those in lower-paying positions. There is a lot of work required to mitigate these types of issues in the private sector. Government agencies appear to have a working grievance procedure that works the majority of the time, although it should be revisited periodically to improve its functional methodology. Performance is a serious matter to employees and there are occasions when overt cases of discrimination and other forms of malfeasance go undetected. In this case, it requires more than a cursory review of the current grievance practices; it may require a complete overhaul to the existing procedures.

Training Action Plans
Chapter Seven

A good way of improving employee performance is by designing training action plans that include individual training needs. Here's what happens: you review an employee's general, technical, and leadership competencies. You find that the employee is lacking in the areas of developing others and problem solving. It is time to design a training action plan to address these deficiencies. If you don't, it is likely that the problem will worsen and the employee will continue to lag or fall short in areas significant to his or her growth in the organization. Some agencies refer to these plans as individual development plans that serve as road maps to guide the administrative and professional careers of those desiring success in their current and future positions. No matter what you call it, design a similar instrument that will serve as a career compass for people to reach maximum success in their job capacities. It is difficult to succeed without one. Also, remember to update action plans annually at a minimum. Action plans also serve as a reminder for managers to reward employees as they accomplish action plan goals. Rewards can take the form of ratings, cash awards, time off awards, and other forms of acknowledgement. Frankly, a certificate noting a particular accomplishment in a performance area is better than nothing at all. Leadership has an obligation to provide the best possible coaching of employees.

Impacting Leadership Competencies
Chapter Eight

For openers, remember that not all employees want to become leaders in the organization. However, for those who do, it is incumbent upon the leadership to make it possible. Whether it is accomplished through leadership development programs or via agency or business intern programs, it is important. The leadership competencies established by the United States Office of Personnel Management (OPM), provide the areas employees should excel in to become good leaders. I suggest visiting www.opm.gov

for additional information. As such, when designing a leadership development program, take into account which areas apply to your employees. Next, define where those areas fit into the structure of your organization. Once this is accomplished, it is advisable to design a program or programs to fit the needs of aspiring leaders within your purview. Agencies use different methods depending on what they are attempting to accomplish. Some who are unsure of where they want to go with a leadership development program rely on private contractors and government agencies that have similar programs in place. Note that however you structure the program, government agencies tend to lean toward the OPM leadership competencies while private agencies may design their own. As I speak with the various training organizations, some use similar approaches while other are vastly different in their efforts to offer best practices in leadership development programs.

The Role of the Trainer
Chapter Nine

A trainer is considered an expert at presenting a particular set of skills to participants who require growth and clarification in a common area of study. The trainer is normally a subject matter expert certified to convey the training materials to increase the knowledge, skills, and abilities of participants.

The trainer may not have the exact certification of those being trained; however, he or she has the wherewithal to present the material successfully and effectively. The ultimate determination of whether a trainer met the goals and objectives of the course rest with the effectiveness of the presentation of the trainer or trainers along with improvements in the employees job performance.

I can think of no profession that requires zero training if people desire to improve their readiness for a particular discipline or job. A trainer is the oil that keeps the lamp burning properly to hold the trainees interest for them to adequately grasp the full intent of the training exercise. One needs the other to promote a productive and viable learning experience. There are certified trainers who do not come across too well as far as some participants are concerned. When this happens, the learning system breaks down. Trainers must practice the art of communication just as much as they rehearse their teaching skills.

There are many keys to a successful learning experience, and adequate communication is one. Without effective communication between the teacher and student, the system breaks down, causing poor or no interaction;

participants cannot receive maximum benefits from the learning experience.

When breakdowns occur, it is usually first reflected in the course evaluation process. Subsequently, participants provide negative feedback verbally, in writing, and through other means. For this reason, trainers must be at their best when training participants at all times.

The Role of the Trainee
Chapter Ten

The trainee is the person on the receiving end of trainers' presentations. Trainees must listen carefully, pay close attention to the other participants, and genuinely concern themselves with the goals and intent of sessions. A good trainee energetically participates in all of the discussions, is not afraid to ask questions, and offers appropriate insight as necessary.

Many training sessions are not as effective as they could be due to trainees' lack of participation. It is not always due to a poor presentation on the part of the trainer. Eager participants who want training to improve in their job capacities will demonstrate a willingness to fully participate in the various aspects of a training course.

When a course goes off track, it is incumbent upon the trainee to help get it back on track by offering comments and suggestions relative to the content of the course. Trainees are more successful when they assist the instructor meet course goals and objectives as opposed to flooding the room with negative criticism. It is the team effort that converts a standard learning experience into a successful and effective learning experience. Students should try hard to ask the questions that clarify things for them. The same question may provide an answer for someone else who may not feel comfortable asking it. Participants should jot down the things they did not ask the instructor due to time constraints or other reasons, and then e-mail them later for a response. Participants should be as honest as they can about the course when filling out the course evaluation, because it serves as the primary improvement tool for the next course as well as the next group of participants.

Overall, effective training solicits the joint responsibility of instructors and participants. One cannot do without the other to realize a true training experience.

Building Capacity
Chapter Eleven

I have heard supervisors and managers say that they have employees who provide little assistance to the team and add no value to the organization. This very statement not only hampers the managers' ability to accomplish their work effectively, it also promotes a negative connotation about the managers' skills. It is important to mention that when managers make such comments it is almost as if they are giving up on those employees. What is important to managers and organizations is what we in managerial circles call "building capacity."

While it may be true that one or more employees lack the ability to make sizable contributions to the team and the organization, it is just as much the mangers' responsibility to reverse the trend by setting developmental goals for employees to build the capacity needed to better perform in their positions. Building capacity takes time and energy, yet it is something that we all must do to get and keep everyone on board, even though it may be to a lesser degree. What happens is that leadership often gives up on employees; they choose not to invest the time required to convert employees who are unable to carry their share of the workload, preferring to support those who learn what they are doing wrong and improve their individual contributions to the team and the organization. Building capacity allows a manager to experience a special appreciation when moving a deadbeat employee to a live participant. This happens when a manager is fully committed to his or her leadership responsibility. Passing responsibility to another manager for a nonperforming employee does not solve the problem.

Sometimes it requires training, counseling, personal improvement plans, and other instruments to get employees on track. The last thing to do is to give up on them as they often bury themselves with doubt and self-pity, which does nothing positive for the team or the organization.

Managers cannot build capacity in an employee without assistance from others in the organization. A primary reason is that it takes a special set of understanding and patience to dive into the inner thoughts of a dysfunctional person and determine how to end nonfunctioning behavior.

If the manager is not willing to take the time to help the employee, it may better to find a willing person who is. The last thing that should be done is to allow a negative performance issue to continue to marinate. When a manager gives the attention needed to resolve the issue, he or she experiences the feeling of accomplishment that comes when a deficient staff person becomes efficient.

There is ample literature and resources on this subject to assist leadership in this regard. I recommend that you review the following books:

Evaluating Training Programs by Donald L. Kirkpatrick,

What is Six Sigma? Pete Pande and Larry Holpp,

10 Steps to Be a Successful Manager, by Lisa Haneberg

ASTD Models for Workplace Learning and Performance: Roles, competencies, and Outputs, by William J. Rothwell, Ethan S. Sanders, and Jeffrey G. Soper

Leading Knowledge Management and Learning (In Action Case Study Series)

Blending E-Learning by Karen Mantyla

Leadership Lessons: 10 Keys to Success in Life & Business by Greg J. Swartz and Julie K. Thorpe

Put Emotional Intelligence to Work: Equip Yourself for Success

Most of these books can be obtained through the American Society for Training and Development. Other industry groups such as Ken Blanchard Companies and the American Management Association can also serve as a good resource for additional career development materials that may be useful in improving Supervisor and Management skills.

Alternative Methods in Training and Development

Chapter Twelve

Undoubtedly, there are times when problems arise within an agency's ability to deliver training to its employees. This is when you search high and low to secure other measures to get the job done irrespective of the problem.

Most problems in the training arena involve the lack of sufficient funding to cover the training needs of the organization. Nevertheless, employees and their agencies expect to have their needs met, as training is designed to improve job performance. How can this happen when there are no funding dollars to pay training vendors and others who implement this particular function?

Well, don't give up...I know of an agency that went four years without the necessary dollars to fund training activities. Instead of complaining and bringing training ambitions to a halt, the agency decided to use in-kind assistance from other training organizations and expanded the use of electronic learning activities. While some employees were against this particular method of training, they learned to appreciate it as a viable alternative. Recognizing that other organizations were in the same boat, the feelings of doom gradually went away. There are times when we are faced with obstacles, particularly in training and development, and we must make adjustments to get the job done. In some cases, the days of extravagant training in plush hotels and conference centers are over. E-training is playing a much larger role in the process. Educational institutions are using more e-learning activities for degree programs than ever before, which may become the norm rather than the exception.

Agencies now reach out to training vendors, taking advantage of group discounts and free admission when possible. Some agencies and businesses have increased their Web casting and video conferencing activities immensely. For now, my guess is that more than 50% of training organizations are using distance learning as the primary mode of communication, particularly government due to tight fiscal constraints, other diminishing training budgets.

Linkages with Training Partners
Chapter Thirteen

Connecting with other training organizations is paramount to the effective delivery of training within the organization. Organizations such as the American Society of Training Development, The Ken Blanchard Companies, SkillSoft, and the American Management Association offer excellent resources to enhance training at the government and private industry levels.

These notable organizations and others provide off-the-shelf courses and instructional design services to assist your organization in meeting your individual training requirements. Some incentives include college-level credit toward various training certifications and certificates for accomplishments in the larger training community. It is recommended that agencies take advantage of the resources offered by other agencies and organizations to broaden their knowledge to better meet locak training needs. Some provide award-winning speakers and seminars to agencies on an as-needed basis. No matter how effective your training programs are, they can improve when exercising an arrangement with external partners. The American Society for Training and Development (ASDT) offers a resource library of training materials to organizations to enhance their knowledge of what other agencies are doing to progress in particular areas of training.

Many schools and universities extend their services by offering graduate and postgraduate programs in human resource development and training. Search the Web and contact some of these groups to see how your organization can take advantage of the services and opportunities offered.

Many provide individual and group memberships to defray costs when scheduling seminar and conference participation. The memberships also assist organizations with special training and certification needs that may be appropriate for your organization.

The Relationship between Human Resources and Training

Chapter Fourteen

In government agencies there is a cross correlation between human resource offices and training. While some operate as separate offices, others merge their training and human resource activities.

Which formulation works better depends on the agency and its overall methods of operation. In some cases, merging the two together stimulates an immediate nexus between two similarly functioning organizations while increasing staff allocations in the sense that the merger can offer up staff from both disciplines as necessary. In other words, if an agency suffers from training staff shortages where human resource staff falls under the same umbrella, agency management can temporarily or permanently reallocate and reassign staff to fulfill critical functions without hiring new staff. In a situation where the two are distinct offices, the shifting of employees and job needs may not be easily accomplished. The Office of Personnel Management normally includes training and human resources together in title and job responsibilities. Some government agencies place their training organizational structure under the office of human resources.

Private companies have the right to structure their training functions as they deem necessary and it is often separate from the human resource function. Normally it depends on the size of the agency and the level of its overall training function.

A police department may require a different type of training compared to a government agency and operate more efficiently under a separate office structure. The standard government structure seems to work best when the offices are combined with separate budget authority. Whatever the structure is, its effectiveness is determined by the extent and types of training provided. Blended learning seems to work well with both private and government agencies, particularly when funding is limited.

Outsourcing Training
Chapter Fifteen

Many agencies find satisfaction in providing and implementing their own internal training programs. For some, this works well and gets the job done. Other organizations prefer to outsource their training needs to private consultants and contractors.

What works well for one organization might not work for another. It is advisable to use a variety of training methods before settling on a standard method of delivery. If an agency has ample staff with the appropriate certifications to train employees in specific areas, it may work to use internal training procedures to accomplish training requirements. If not, it may be time to use the outsourcing method by having private contractors take responsibility for your training needs. Private contractors shine a different light on the organization, as they can be more objective in their strategies to meet your internal training requirements.

Additionally, they may offer resources that your agency does not have or simply can't afford, such as updated technology. As agencies experience downsizing and staff shortages, private contracting is likely the better way to go. However, it is important to procure contractors with reputations that complement the overall training goals of the organization. Contractors who perform poorly should not be considered during the outsourcing process.

Using the approach of some internal training along with external support may be a good way of adding variety to the needs of the organization.

Making Training a Success
for All Parties
Chapter Sixteen

Training seems more successful when the concept of teaming occurs. For example, one agency formed task forces and groups to outline annual training needs for the agency. Afterward, they hired private contractors to review their plans and conduct the training. The employees enjoyed it, as they got the chance to join the contractors during some of the external sessions.

It was a way of vesting the agency employees while securing invaluable learning from industry experts. In cases where external partners were unfamiliar with the office structure of the agency, the internal employees were minimizing breakdowns in communication during training exercises. It seems to work when an agency involves all parties to a training agreement from start to finish. Internal and external partnering can lead to a fully objective and successful training experience.

Training Do's and Don'ts
Chapter Seventeen

- When devising your training plan, include participants in the planning.
- When planning training strategies, include internal and external partners.
- When including partners, ensure that you have the right ones.
- When you have the right partners, be objective with one another and give credence to each other's ideas.
- When deciding on a location for training, consider all factors including transportation issues, meals, hotel costs, equipment, and comfort.

- When scheduling training, consider important factors such as inclement weather, time of the year (e.g., holidays), and size of the facility.
- When selecting instructors, review their previous participation with other agencies and groups.
- When outsourcing training, be vigilant about past performance issues and concerns with the prospective contractor.
- When devising the training agenda, allow others to review it prior to implementation.
- When training is completed, ensure that you collect as many training evaluations as possible and follow up with responses to trainee questions and concerns that could not be answered during the session.

Training Modules
Chapter Eighteen

A good training course contains a module outlining each area that will be covered during the course. The modules should be clear and cover all aspects of the content of each one. They should be divided, placed in a binder or similar document file, and followed verbatim throughout the delivery of the course.

Training modules make it easier for the instructor to stay on track with the course content while giving trainees something to view as they follow the instructor's pace, as governed by the training agenda. It is advisable not to deviate from the training module as some trainees become confused or lose sight of the content when deviation occurs. Modules are significant to learners' ability to revisit each item after course hours and following completion.

Modules indeed provide a road map to accomplish the intent and purpose of the training while allowing students and trainees to navigate along with the instructor and fellow trainees. It is recommended that trainees review the training modules before, during, and after course completion for clarity and inconsistencies

All inconsistencies should be shared with the instructor for correction. Training modules are among the best tools used in communicating course content during training activities.

Training Best Practices
Chapter Nineteen

It has been stated that one of the best practices in training occurs when there is pure and obvious interaction between the instructor and student. Courses that exclude clear interaction between the two do not exemplify a training best practice. Interaction evokes a caring participation between two parties required to demonstrate a viable learning sequence. While learning can take place without interaction, it is not as effective as the practice of mutual involvement. This deficiency can be addressed in a number of ways. One, the instructor can use techniques that automatically engage participants, including assigning team leaders and spokespersons and giving each participant a specific role in the training process. Secondly, each trainee can be given a number that represents a time for them to respond to a particular question or comment raised by the instructor. Thirdly, the trainee can offer suggestions to the instructor that engages the participants in a mutually desirable fashion. The bottom line is to promote full participation in the learning process; these are a few ways to get it going.

Some instructors and trainers feel confident elaborating on their training presentation with minimal or no input from the participants. This is not good. Compassionate trainers prefer a give-and-take relationship between them and the audience during the training process. Compassion makes participants feel vested in the purpose of the session as well as allowing them to express their feelings and concerns while they are fresh in their minds.

Waiting for participants to express their thoughts and comments at the end of the session is not as effective if effective at all. As a matter of fact, there is evidence that when participants do not become mutually involved in the learning segment, they tend to become disinterested and sometimes do not return to the session. Think what would happen if every participant in a training session did this—there would be no one to train.

There is a big difference between classroom and electronic training. Electronic training permits trainees to move at their own pace within incremental time frames, the complete opposite of classroom training. When a trainer is bound by a training module and time constraints, there is little flexibility to change things.

What gives a positive attribute to electronic or e-training courses is the self-paced option that is built into the learning sequence. Mutual interaction rarely occurs in the e-training process, although the voiced narrative you hear serves as an instructor-led session. The fact is that you can't ask questions or make comments in most electronic learning methods. But you can improve your understanding by taking the course more than once until you are satisfied with your final score.

Classroom training tends not to place so much emphasis on testing, which is preferred by trainees who don't do well with written tests, particularly in the presence of other people. While there are pros and cons to both training methods, the ultimate goal is to offer the opportunity for employees to improve their skills by understanding the roles and responsibilities of their jobs.

Mentoring and coaching can serve as another form of training. A mentor agrees to accept an employee as his or her responsibility to work with in various areas of career development activities. The same is true for a coach. A coach takes responsibility for an employee by developing and tracking the individual progress of a protégé on a regularly scheduled basis. While mentoring provides general career support to employees, coaching is more specific and tends to operate at a higher level, usually by a supervisor or manager. If done correctly, this method of training can boost the morale of employees while instilling in them the elements of learning behaviors that can make them more successful at what they do in their job capacities. It is not as costly as other forms of training and can normally be accomplished within the agency.

External coaching is available through several organizations in the human resource and training industry.

Training Evaluations
Chapter Twenty

There are several ways to evaluate the results of the training received by a business or government agency. One popular method is contained in the book Evaluating Training Programs by Donald L. Kirkpatrick. He uses four levels of evaluation: reaction, learning, behavior, and results, which I covered earlier.

However, a business or government agency can develop its own methods of evaluating employee training activities. You may want to consider using a summary of what a trainer noticed about a participant throughout the course. The problem with this is that it would be one-sided. Again, learning is a two-part process between a trainer and a trainee.

Consequently, an instructor's evaluation alone would not tell how a trainee felt about the course. To rectify this, it's essential to receive specific comments from a trainee about the training and how it affected him or her. A one-page form is used in some cases to capture training feedback, which is acceptable if it asks substantive questions and leaves room for related comments.

If not, an agency of government or business should pursue developing an evaluation process that will provide a better understanding of employees. A catastrophe occurs when there is no evaluation process at all.

Another important aspect of the evaluation process is how the agency plans to track its employee training for periods of time. Should the agency use an automated tracking system or is a general spreadsheet sufficient? Tracking training is big business, as it tells you the extent of an employee's learning history, which, in some cases, can be the deciding factor in job placement and promotions.

Whatever system is used, it should be effectively maintained by more than one person if possible. Invariably, it is the day that the training records person is out when a manager or supervisor needs information on an employee's training record.

Training Locations
Chapter Twenty-One

When searching for a training facility, contact other private and government organizations before making a final decision. There are facilities in most locations throughout the nation that provide the fundamentals required for a satisfactory training experience. Also, as cost is always an important factor, you will be surprised at the differences between one facility and another. With shrinking financial reserves, particularly in the area of training, it pays to get the best offer available.

If you choose to use Web casting, videoconferencings, and other forms of electronic learning, make sure that all equipment is working properly. It saves embarrassment for the trainer, trainee, and the agency. Again, always keep adequate records on agency training activities.

Training Summary
Chapter Twenty-Two

A good training plan has the following ingredients:

Defining the problem – The first step sets the stage for the project as a whole and often poses the greatest challenge to a team. The team must grapple with an array of questions about what they are working on, why, who should lead the charge, and what the benefits are for making the improvements.

Analyze – Whether you utilize a needs assessment or another instrument to determine the training needs for your agency, this must be done. The assessment should be designed to show each employee working for the business or agency with a plan to address and improve potential skill gaps within each employee's job capacities. It is important to know the training history, including courses taken outside the agency irrespective of who paid for them. Carefully review what is required for each employee's position in terms of which competencies apply and which ones do not.

Improve – The business or agency must decide the best method of providing training to improve each employee's job skills while determining the impact training may have in terms of costs, time away from the office, and how a position fits into the total staffing structure of the agency or business.

Controls – Controls must be put in place to maintain positive momentum as the employee begins to grow and further develop the job skills required for his or her current and future position. The skills must be tracked with accurate records that correspond with the employee's actual training accomplishments. Without internal controls, businesses and agencies lose touch with valuable information on the career development activities of the employees.

Review and follow-up – The human resource and training staff should periodically review employee training against career growth and development. The business or agency is successful when the employee training plan has directly or indirectly increased an employee's growth within the organization as reflected in better performance ratings or promotions. If the review and follow-up are stagnant, other arrangements should be made to get the employee back on track. This may include reassigning the employee to a different position, one that he or she is more appropriately qualified for, and it should be done based on evaluations of growth and development.

Acknowledgements

This book is dedicated to every hard-working trainer and human resource professional out there. Managing human resources and training cannot be taken lightly, for it matches people with jobs and gives them a base through training programs to improve their skills while managing their talents.

Keep making them happy. And to all those managers and supervisors, when you need a quick fix on employee development pick up this book and use it as a guide. It offers a large amount of information in a small number of pages.

For group sales, distribution and inquiries call Innovative Ventures, Incorporated at 703 407-2325.

Reginald Hayes is available for speeches and workshops.   Contact www.reginaldhayes.com or e-mail rbhayes1967@aol.com

For more information about Innovative Ventures Incorporated visit www.innovativeventuresgroup.com